Reading Roundabout

# My Day

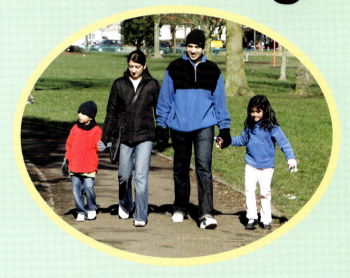

Paul Humphrey

Photography by Chris Fairclough

**W**

**FRANKLIN WATTS**

LONDON • SYDNEY

First published in 2005 by
Franklin Watts
96 Leonard Street
London EC2A 4XD

Franklin Watts Australia
Level 17/207 Kent Street
Sydney NSW 2000

ISBN 0 7496 6181 X (hbk)
ISBN 0 7496 6193 3 (pbk)

Dewey classification number: 529'.1

A CIP catalogue record for this book is available
from the British Library.

Planning and production by Discovery Books Limited
Editor: Rachel Tisdale
Designer: Ian Winton
Photography: Chris Fairclough
Series advisors: Diana Bentley MA and Dee Reid MA,
Fellows of Oxford Brookes University

The author, packager and publisher would like to thank the following people
for their participation in this book: Kam, Suki and Arrandeep Bola, and
Anusha Joshi.

Printed in China

12 - 2011

# Contents

# It's Saturday. There is no school today.

What shall I do?

5

6

Now let's play with my game.

15

16

Now we can go for a walk.

19

21

22

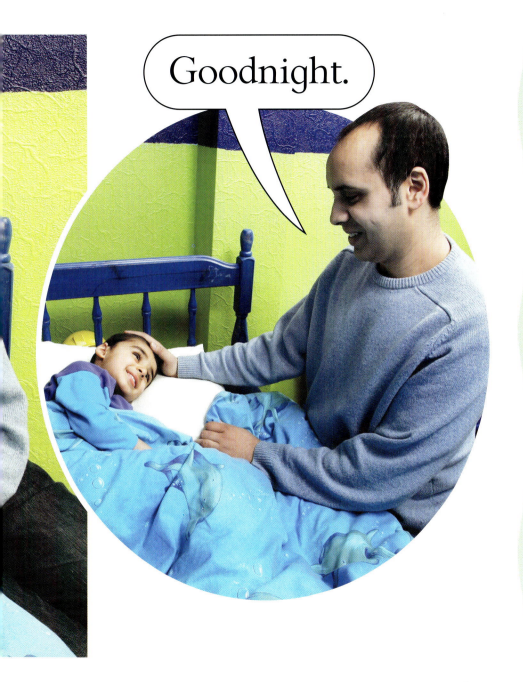

23

# Word bank

Look back for these words and pictures.

### Dressing up

### Game

### Garden

### Hide

### Juice

### Lunch

### Pizza

### Play

### Walk